COOL
BIOLOGICAL
CLUES

What Hair, Bones, and Bugs Tell Us

ESTHER BECK

ABDO
Publishing Company

VISIT US AT WWW.ABDOPUBLISHING.COM

Published by ABDO Publishing Company, 8000 West 78th Street, Edina, Minnesota 55439.
Copyright © 2009 by Abdo Consulting Group, Inc. International copyrights reserved in all countries.
No part of this book may be reproduced in any form without written permission from the publisher.
The Checkerboard Library™ is a trademark and logo of ABDO Publishing Company.

Printed in the United States.
Design and Production: Mighty Media, Inc.
Art Direction: Kelly Doudna
Photo Credits: Kelly Doudna, Ablestock, iStockPhoto (Justin Horrocks, Daniel Mathys),
Peter Arnold Inc. (Biosphoto/Tristan Da Cunha, Ed Reschke), ShutterStock
Series Editor: Pam Price

Library of Congress Cataloging-in-Publication Data

Beck, Esther.
   Cool biological clues : what hair, bones, and bugs tell us / Esther
Beck.
      p. cm. -- (Cool CSI)
   Includes index.
   ISBN 978-1-60453-483-2
   1. Forensic sciences--Juvenile literature. 2. Evidence, Criminal--
Juvenile literature. 3. Crime scene searches--Juvenile literature.
4. Criminal investigation--Juvenile literature. I. Title.

   HV8073.8.B424 2008
   363.25'62--dc22

                              2008023808

TO ADULT HELPERS

You're invited to assist up-and-coming forensic investigators! And it will pay off in many ways. Your children can develop new skills, gain confidence, and do some interesting projects while learning about science. What's more, it's going to be a lot of fun!

These projects are designed to let children work independently as much as possible. Let them do whatever they are able to do on their own. Also encourage them to keep a CSI journal. Soon, they will be thinking like real investigators.

So get out your magnifying glass and stand by. Let your young investigators take the lead. Watch and learn. Praise their efforts. Enjoy the scientific adventure!

CONTENTS

fingerprint

shoe print

fibers

FUN WITH FORENSICS

So you want to know more about crime scene investigation, or CSI. Perhaps you saw a crime solvers show on television and liked it. Or maybe you read about an ace investigator in a favorite **whodunit** book. Now you're curious, how do the investigators solve crimes?

The answer is *forensic science*. This term means science as it relates to the law. The many areas of forensic science can help link people to crimes, even if there are no eyewitnesses. Forensic scientists look at the evidence left at a crime scene and try to figure out what happened there.

tool marks

DNA sample

chemical residue

Evidence can include fingerprints, shoe prints, and fibers. It can include DNA samples from blood and saliva, tool marks, and chemical residue. Often this evidence can be quite small. In the CSI business, this is known as trace evidence. But even the smallest evidence can place a suspect at a crime scene.

Crime scene investigators **analyze** the evidence. Then they try to answer these questions about a crime.

1. What happened?
2. Where and when did it occur?
3. Who are the suspects, and why did they do it?
4. How was the crime done?

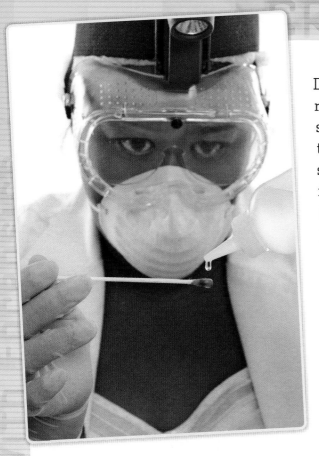

Different kinds of evidence require different kinds of scientists to find the answers to these questions. Forensic scientists specialize in fields such as chemistry, biology, physics, engineering, psychology, and even **entomology** and **botany**.

All these scientists use common sense and old-fashioned observation. They also rely on high-tech equipment and the latest scientific discoveries. Most important, forensic scientists use the scientific method.

Investigators begin by observing the crime scene. They then predict what happened and, if possible, who committed the crime based on the evidence.

Next they test the evidence. Their test results may support their predictions. Or, the results may tell them that their predictions were not correct.

Finally, they draw a conclusion about what happened. They may decide that further testing is required.

In this book series, you'll have a chance to test your own crime-solving talent. You'll do some challenging hands-on forensics activities. Each book in the series covers a specific area of CSI. In addition to this book, *Cool Biological Clues: What Hair, Bones, and Bugs Tell Us*, be sure to check out:

- *Cool Crime Scene Basics: Securing the Scene*
- *Cool Eyewitness Encounters: How's Your Memory?*
- *Cool Forensic Tools: Technology at Work*
- *Cool Physical Evidence: What's Left Behind*
- *Cool Written Records: The Proof Is in the Paper*

Altogether, these books show how crime scene investigators use science to **analyze** evidence and solve crimes.

Whoduzit in Whodunits: Forensic Psychologists

Psychologists study minds and behavior. Forensic psychologists study the minds and behavior of crime suspects. They try to determine motive, or why a person may have committed a crime. They may try to determine whether a person was sane when he or she committed a crime.

F211A

CSI LAB

The Scientific Method

Forensic scientists aren't the only ones who use the scientific method. All scientists do.

The scientific method is a series of steps that scientists follow when trying to answer a question about how the world works. Here are the basic steps of the scientific method.

1. Observe. Pay attention to how something works.

2. Predict. Make a simple statement that explains what you observed.

3. Test. Design an experiment that tests your prediction. You need a good idea of what data to gather during the test. A good test has more than one trial and has controlled variables.

4. Conclude. Compare the data and make a conclusion. This conclusion should relate to your prediction. It will either support the prediction or tell you that your prediction was incorrect.

COOL CSI JOURNAL

Taking notes is important when you collect evidence as a crime scene investigator. Writing down facts helps crime scene investigators remember all the details of a crime scene later, when a crime is tried in court.

At the beginning of each activity in this book, there is a section called "Take Note!" It contains suggestions about what to record in your CSI journal. You

can predict what you think will happen when you test evidence. And you can write down what did happen. Then you can draw a conclusion.

As you do experiments, record things in your journal. You will be working just like a real forensic scientist.

TAKE NOTE!

Get out your CSI journal when you see this box. "Take Note!" may have questions for you to answer about the project. There may be a suggestion about how to look at the project in a different way. There may even be ideas about how to organize the evidence you find. Your CSI journal is the place to keep track of everything!

SAFE SCIENCE

Good scientists practice safe science. Here are some important things to remember.

- **Check with an adult** before you begin any project. Sometimes you'll need an adult to buy materials or help you handle them for a while. For some projects, an adult will need to help you the whole time. The instructions will say when an adult should assist you.

- **Ask for help** if you're unsure about how to do something.

- If something goes wrong, **tell an adult** immediately.

- **Read the list** of things you'll need. Gather everything before you begin working on a project.

- **Don't taste, eat, or drink** any of the materials or the results unless the directions say that you can.

- **Use protective gear.** Scientists wear safety goggles to protect their eyes. They wear gloves to protect their hands from chemicals and possible burns. They wear aprons or lab coats to protect their clothing.

- **Clean up** when you are finished. That includes putting away materials and washing containers, work surfaces, and your hands.

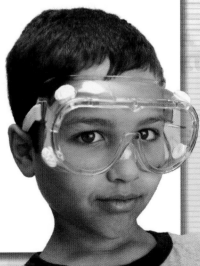

COOL BIOLOGICAL CLUES: WHAT HAIR, BONES, AND BUGS TELL US

Scientists can use what they know about nature to help solve crimes. It's a fascinating business!

Biology is the study of plants and animals. This field of science informs crime solvers. It's all about where and how living things grow. In the crime world, biological evidence is anything that is organic, or occurs in nature. Blood, hair, bones, plant pollen and seeds, and common insects are a few examples.

Take a minute to think about hair, a very common biological clue. Human beings shed about 100 hairs each and every day. It's no wonder that strands show up at crime scenes. An individual hair can point investigators on their way to solving a crime. It can help them narrow a field of suspects based on its color, length, and texture.

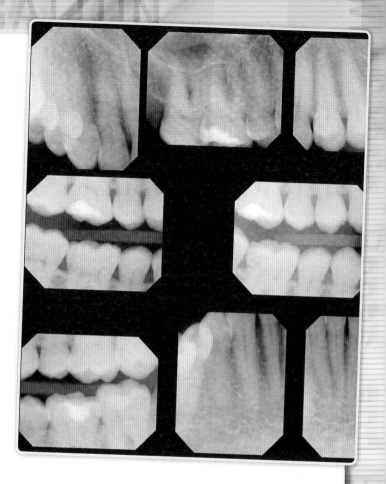

Teeth can also provide biological clues. Sometimes a crime scene includes human remains that cannot be identified. Investigators try to match the teeth they find with dental records to name the victim. Similarly, bones can reveal the sex and age of a victim. They can even suggest the race of a victim.

Animals besides humans can also provide biological evidence. Insects as tiny as flies are used to estimate the time of death of victims. That's because insects go through metamorphosis.

That means they change form over their life spans.
Scientists can estimate time based on these changes.
Good thinking!

Plant science, or **botany**, is another important source of
biological evidence. Nearly 300,000 species of plants have
been identified around the world. Scientists use what they
know about the green world to solve crimes. They identify
pollen and other plant parts that appear at a crime scene.
These can help place a suspect at the scene.

None of the evidence described above needs to be very large to provide a big break in a **case**. Trace evidence is evidence that is found in small amounts. Biological evidence can be small, but still very important.

The activities in this book all center around biological evidence. So roll up your sleeves. Learning how forensic scientists put the natural world to work to solve crimes is good science fun!

POLLEN POLICE

THE CRIME SCENE: One of your cats knocks over a big vase of flowers. Your mom suspects Fluffy, who likes to jump on the table. But you think that Fluffy should remain innocent until proven guilty.

Pollen is a fine powder that plants use to reproduce. So you examine all of the cats for pollen in their fur. What will your botanical **sleuthing** reveal?

THINK CSI

Pollen is really handy for investigators because it's so small. Criminals don't try to destroy this evidence because they can't see it! But if a suspect has pollen or seeds from the crime scene on his or her clothes, it could prove that he or she was there. Investigators often rely on forensic botanists to study plant evidence.

1. Shake the pollen from each kind of flower or pine cone onto its own piece of black paper.

2. Look at each pollen sample with a magnifying glass or a microscope.

3. Use your CSI journal to track how each pollen sample looks.

TAKE NOTE!

Sketch and describe the pollen samples in your CSI journal. Use a chart similar to the one shown below. Think how these notes might come in handy when solving a crime.

Name of flower or pine cone	Color of pollen	Shape of pollen

Whoduzit in Whodunits: Forensic Botanist

A **botanist** is a scientist who studies plants. Forensic botanists apply what they know about plants to help solve crimes. Once plants are found as evidence, forensic botanists are called in. Their scientific knowledge is very specific. Most crime investigators simply don't know enough about plants to **analyze** them. You could say that it's not easy seeing green!

INSECT INVESTIGATOR

THE CRIME SCENE: Tiny tan-and-black flies with red eyes have invaded your kitchen! A neighbor says they look like *Drosophila melanogaster*. He explains that something in the kitchen is attracting them. Time to put on your **entomology** hat! Can you figure out what's inviting to these small flies with the big name?

Observe the complete life cycle of the common fruit fly. All you need are some everyday materials, a grown-up assistant, and a few weeks.

MATERIALS

- quart jar
- banana
- cloth for lid, such as a nylon stocking
- rubber band

1. Peel the banana and place the fruit in the jar.

2. Leave the jar open for 12 to 24 hours. Be sure to place it in the shade if the weather is warm.

1

TAKE NOTE!

The life cycle of a common fruit fly has four stages. Look for these stages as you watch your flies grow.

1. Eggs. Fruit flies will lay eggs on the banana. The eggs are light in color and may be hard to see. If they are, put a piece of black paper under or inside the jar.

2. Larvae. White, wormlike **larvae** hatch and grow to approximately ⅛ inch (3.2 mm) in length. Larvae are sometimes called maggots.

3. Pupae. Eight or nine days after the eggs are laid, the larval skin hardens to form **pupae**, which look like tiny cigars.

4. Adult flies. Flies emerge from the pupae two weeks after the eggs are laid. They live for about two weeks. During that time, they find mates and lay the next generation of eggs.

Be sure to keep detailed notes of your observations. What did you learn about fruit flies that you didn't know before?

eggs

larva

pupa

adult fly

3. Check the jar a couple of times a day to see whether the rotting fruit has attracted any flies.

4. When you see flies on the banana, carefully cover the jar with the cloth. Then secure it with a rubber band.

5. Watch the flies as they go through their life cycle. You don't have to do anything to take care of them except moisten the banana if it dries out.

6. See the "Take Note!" section on page 19 for a description of the life cycle of fruit flies.

CSI Tip

No luck catching flies? *Drosophila melanogaster*, also known as fruit flies, can be purchased from biological supply companies, such as Carolina Biological Supply Company (www.carolina.com).

Insect Investigator

Whoduzit in Whodunits: Forensic Entomologist

It might seem odd that people who study bugs can help solve crimes. But forensic **entomologists** can answer crime puzzlers such as the approximate time of death of a victim. That's because insects go through metamorphosis, or a change in form, as they develop. Entomologists look for certain flies at crime scenes. Then they estimate how long these insects have been around. This process gives a whole new meaning to watching a bug's life!

GET THE DIRT!

THE CRIME SCENE: Your dad is mad! Somebody tracked dirt and mud through the house, and he wants to know **whodunit.** Luckily, he's an avid mystery reader. So he knows that dirt and dust are common ways to catch a criminal. Are you in trouble? Find out when your dad gets the dirt!

Dirt and dust can link a suspect to a crime scene. In this activity, you'll **analyze** dirt to try to make a match.

MATERIALS

- soil samples from six sites
- plastic bags
- pen or marker
- white paper
- magnifying glass

TAKE NOTE!

Make a table of your results, using one row for each soil sample. Describe each sample. What color is the dirt? Are there rocks in it? Are the grains large or small? Do you see any plant matter in the sample? Can you see how forensic scientists can use dirt as evidence?

1. Collect dirt, or soil, from six different locations. Take your samples from the surface.

2. Place each sample in a separate plastic bag and label it with the sample location.

3. Pour a small amount of one soil sample onto a piece of paper.

4. Examine the soil with a magnifying glass.

5. Write what you see in your CSI journal. Read the "Take Note!" section to get ideas about what to look for.

2

BACKYARD

3

BACKYARD

4

CSI TIP

Investigators use vacuums to collect trace evidence such as dirt. They vacuum near the area where they know the criminal had to have been. The most useful dirt is the kind that can prove a person was at the scene. For example, when a certain kind of dirt was found on the suspect's shoes and this same kind of dirt appears at the crime scene, you could say the inspectors hit pay dirt!

HAIR COMPARE

THE CRIME SCENE: At school, your music teacher's favorite ukulele has disappeared. She has no idea what happened to it. So she checks the room for clues and spies a hair near the instrument shelf. Could this tiny bit of evidence help solve the Mystery of the Lost Ukulele?

Hair **analysis** is a common forensic test. In this activity, you'll study hairs from different sources. And, you'll learn more about how a simple hair compare can help solve crimes.

MATERIALS

- hair samples from different people. Ask them to pull single hairs for you or to take samples from their brushes.
- hair samples from pets. You can collect these from a piece of furniture or a pet brush.
- white paper or index cards
- pen
- tape
- magnifying glass or microscope
- microscope slide and cover slip (optional)

TAKE NOTE!

Draw a sketch of what you see when you look at each hair up close. Describe each sample, noting its length, color, and texture. How are the samples alike? How are they different? How does human hair compare with pet hair?

1. Tape each hair sample to a piece of paper or an index card.

2. Label each sample with the person or animal's name.

3. View each sample up close, using the magnifying glass or the microscope.

4. For extra fun, get a second sample from your "suspects." Tape these samples as before, but hide the labels on the backs of the cards.

5. Mix up the second set of samples. Then try to match the two sets. Is it easy to determine which hairs are from the same person? How about from the same pet?

CSI TIP

Hair is commonly found at a crime scene and gathered as evidence. But it's not what experts call conclusive evidence. Using microscopes alone, investigators can't say for sure that the hair belongs to a specific person. But the results can help narrow the field. And **analyzing** hair is fast and easy to do.

There is one way that hair can be used as direct evidence. Have you heard of DNA? This is the genetic code that each of us has in our cells. If a hair is broken off or cut, it is not a good source of DNA. But if a hair is pulled out at its root, scientists can use the root to test DNA. This test makes it possible to match the hair to a single suspect.

Think CSI

When you view hair under a microscope, look for three parts.

1. Cuticle. This is the see-through outer covering that looks like scales.

2. Cortex. This is the main part of the hair.

3. Medulla. This is the hair's inner core, which features a **unique** pattern. Scientists look at the medulla to determine what kind of animal the hair comes from.

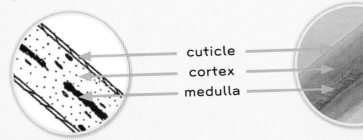

cuticle
cortex
medulla

EVEN MORE TO EXPLORE

If you have access to a microscope, try making a wet mount of a hair. You'll need a microscope slide and a cover slip.

1. Put a couple drops of water on the center of the slide.

2. Lay the hair on the slide, curving it to place both the root and the tip in the water.

3. Place the cover slip over the hair and the water. To do this, position the slip on its edge next to the area you want to cover. Then gently ease it into place, trying not to disturb the sample.

4. Take a look at the sample under the microscope. How does this view of a hair compare with the sample on white paper?

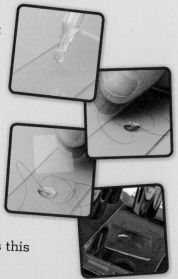

ANALYZING AN OWL PELLET

MATERIALS

- owl pellet. You can buy one from a science company, such as www.pellet.com.
- bone identification chart, which is also available at www.pellet.com
- disposable aluminum cake pan
- magnifying glass
- tweezers
- latex gloves
- antibacterial soap

THE CRIME SCENE: Your neighbors are remodeling. Underneath the front porch they find the skeleton of a small animal! You like a good mystery. So you ask if you can study the bones. What small critter died here?

Sometimes a crime scene is found long after the crime occurs. Sometimes it involves fire or other extreme conditions. Crime solvers can use teeth and bones to figure out who the victims were long after the fact. In this activity, you'll dissect an owl pellet, which is the parts of a bird's food that can't be digested. Then you'll try to identify the small animal bones in the pellet.

TAKE NOTE!

Draw and label the bones you find in your owl pellet. Compare your sketches with sketches your friends make. How do the contents of your owl pellets compare?

Birds **regurgitate** the parts of food they can't digest. Owl pellets often contain parts of the animals the birds ate. Bones, bills, claws, teeth, and even fur and feathers can be found in pellets. Take a look and see what you find in your pellet.

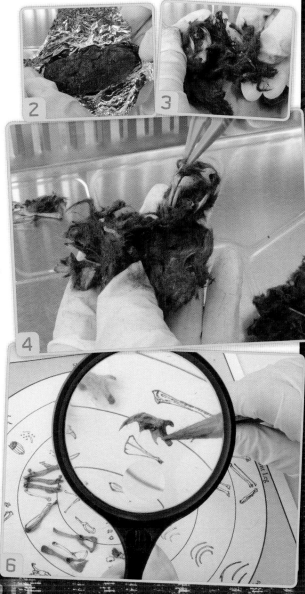

1. Put on your latex gloves.

2. Open the pellet foil and place the contents of the package in the disposable aluminum cake pan.

3. Using your hands, gently break apart the pellet.

4. Use the tweezers to select any bones you see. Place them on the paper.

5. When you've removed all the bones, use the magnifying glass to study them.

6. Compare the bones in your pellet with those in the bone identification chart. Try to identify the parts of the animals in the pellet.

7. Throw away the cake pan, the contents of the pellet, and your gloves.

8. Wash the tweezers and your hands with warm water and antibacterial soap.

Whoduzit in Whodunits: Forensic Anthropologist

Physical anthropologists study fossils to learn more about how human beings lived. When anthropologists use their skills to help solve crimes, they are called forensic anthropologists.

THINK CSI

Teeth are another way that forensic scientists identify victims. They compare the remains with dental records to help make a match.

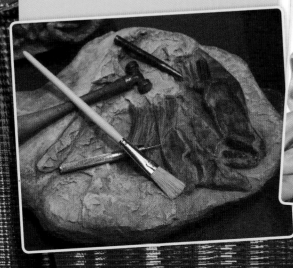

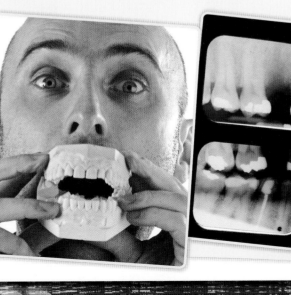

CONCLUSION

The activities found in this book are not complicated. But real-life crime scenes can be. Solving crimes using biological clues requires that investigators know their subject matter backward and forward. Then they can apply it creatively to crack complicated **cases**.

Now that you know the basics of how forensic scientists use biological clues, pay attention! Next time you read a mystery, look for clues that are found in nature. Human beings, plants, animals, and bugs are all fair game.

Scientists study the way the world works. When you have a question, look up the answer or ask your science teacher. Forensic scientists use resources too. It's all part of the job!

GLOSSARY

analysis – the identification or study of the parts of a whole.

analyze – to study the parts of something to discover how it works or what it means.

botany – the study of plants.

case – a situation requiring investigation and consideration by police. Also, the set of arguments made by a lawyer in a court of law.

entomology – the study of bugs.

larva – a newly hatched wingless insect, before it transforms. *Larvae* is the plural of *larva*.

pupa – the stage when an insect transforms from a larva to an adult. *Pupae* is the plural of *pupa*.

regurgitate – to bring food that has already been swallowed back into the mouth.

sleuth – to act like a detective and search for information.

unique – being the only one of its kind.

whodunit – a slang word meaning detective story or mystery story.

WEB SITES

To learn more about the science of forensics, visit ABDO Publishing Company on the World Wide Web at www.abdopublishing.com. Web sites about CSI and forensics are featured on our Book Links page. These links are routinely monitored and updated to provide the most current information available.

INDEX